a Night
w i t h o u t armor II:
the revenge

a Night without armor II: the revenge

Poems

Beau Sia

mouth
almighty
books

THIS BOOK IS DEDICATED TO
  my family (mom, dad, may-lee, melody),
  my friends,
  the north wind, the merits of failure, pizza,
  bad writers, the chinese
  weapons that are out of vogue,
  enlightening heart attacks,
  joan jett, cuddly bears, all things blue, and the land
  which brings erection
  with every whisper of its name
  in the sacred cavern
  that is
  my melancholious heart: oklahoma.

First Edition

Cover Photos by Ill Badler

ISBN.0-9662042-9

contents

dear jewel

I am writing this letter to thank you for your book of poetry. *A Night Without Armor* has been so inspirational to me that I've written an entire book of poems in four hours called *A Night Without Armor II: The Revenge*. They have the same titles as your poems, but they are entirely different poems. My mother likes our books, but I think that she prefers your poetry over mine, though she tells me that she likes mine more. I guess a mother's love has no boundaries. I also let one of my sisters read my book and she said it was hilarious. Can you believe it? I hope that the rest of the opinions I get on my book are just as good. I get really depressed when people say bad or mediocre things about my work. There was this review in a magazine about my upcoming spoken word CD *Attack! Attack! Go!,* and it said that I was good with expletives, like it's a compliment. I thought it was a general way of saying that I don't have any artistic merit and that I have fallen back on shock value. I'm deep, really I am. In fact, I often ask myself many deep questions like, "What is happiness?," "Is there beauty in the ugliness of life?" "Why does love hurt?," and "Does truth exist in the eyes of a liar?" Do you ever ask yourself those kind of questions? I feel like you do, because in your songs that I hear on the radio, I notice that there's a struggle inside you to get to the heart of the matter with all of life's challenging questions. I used to challenge myself every day with writing. I thought Charles Bukowski was the best and that everything he said was gold, so when I read that he wrote ten pages a day, I decided that I was going to do the same thing. Those were my prolific days. Now I don't write except when I have to for a performance or a submission to a magazine or something. I'm not saying that I perform all the time or that I'm in every major literary publication, because I am not that famous yet. Hopefully I won't be famous and I'll just be rich. That way I can enjoy a very private life filled with excessiveness like bathing in maple syrup and marshmallows.

I hope you like my book. I think if we ever meet that we'd be great friends. In fact, we already have some things in common. You're from Alaska and I'm from Oklahoma. Both of these states end with the letter "a." I can see a very bright future ahead for us. Oh, this letter is also doubling as a preface to my book. Anyway, I'm going to stop writing, because I want my girlfriend to give me hickies right now, so that I can tell people that I was attacked by a bear.

Yours in poetry,

as a child I walked

through mazes
made of
couch cushions.

I called myself an explorer.

senor fuckface,
walking
in search of
a new world.

in the hallway
between the kitchen
and my mother's bedroom
I learned that
this
poem sucks.

the bony ribs of adam

I was never
very religious.

in catholic school
I would promise
the priest
that if I ever won
the lottery
I would donate $100,000
to the church.

I thought this would
soften
him up.

communion never
fulfilled me.

confession was not
confession.

the only thing
I've ever confirmed
has been
that I can do
just fine
on my own.

but thank you jesus
for pleated skirts.

wild horse

if I close my eyes
I can remember
the first time
we had sex.

I've blocked
the memory
into
the category
of 'screamers.'

too bad
an insatiable
bed manner
does not equate
to
a crazy
outlook
on life.

if we were still
seeing each other
I'd shake you
and say,

"stop being so reserved!
do you know
what year it is?!"

I would have
traded
every orgasm
with you
for a day
in the park
with kimchee.

boring
will not
bring on
anything.

bukowsky's widow

I'm certain
that if he had
only lived
for another
year
I would have
met him.

every time
an
influential writer dies
in america,
I get thoughts.

how will the body
of my work be viewed
in the eyes
of the public
once I am dead?

how many books
will they publish
out of
the poems I couldn't stand?

you tell me

that there are
two reasons
why
we can't have sex
right now.

a. thoughts of boyfriend
    plaguing your brain.
b. I do not have a condom.

lying naked
on my bed,
I put on a condom
and we
learn
about each other
for the rest
of the night.

in the morning
you leave.

I sleep,
dreaming
of
possibility.

paramount, ny,

right now
I'm trying
to astral project myself
to this place
and time
so that
I can
catch
the naked jewel
mentioned in the
same titled poem
as this.

I am unsuccessful.

it does not
matter.

it has been long

since
I sat on my porch
in oklahoma,
next to _____,
talking
about love.

since
someone has told me,
"I love you,"
besides
my mother.

since
the challenger crash
and elementary school
fear.

since
I woke up
empowered.

too many nights

I could be fucking
all the time.

but I'm used to
the daily routine.

I love writing!

I look at young girls now

I sleep with
twentysomethings now.

the days of reading lolita
for me
are over.

naomi was
a book
of nostalgia.

...young girls possess
so many qualities
that make me want to
date them,
fuck them,
marry them, marry them.

and I could spend
more pages
on
the subject.

but it all comes down to
this:

I do not
want
that advantage
anymore.

young girls be free.

seattle

in the days of grunge
I joined
a garage band
with my best friend.

after a few rehearsals
they told me
that I was
out of the band,
because
they did not need
a second drummer.

I knew all along
that it
really was because
I'm chinese.

white america
is afraid of
the chinese percussionist.

saved from myself

I once stopped
myself
from
committing
suicide.

I treated myself
to a banana split
and
a porno
afterwards.

taking the slave

she likes to be
choked
in bed.

the price
of violent sex
is the distance
in her eyes
when she's sober.

heroin
makes

connecting

hard.

sun bathing

I used to get
a great tan line
during summers
on the
swim team.

now I have
a stupid
trunks line.

if only speedos
were more
socially
acceptable
in the U.S.
of A.

red roof inn, boston

I have yet to
sleep with
a woman
while staying
in boston.

next time I'm there,
I'll probably
have to
take some
devoted fan
to the
red roof inn.

then,
in the 2nd edition
of this book,
I'll really have
a poem
that fits
this title.

so just kiss me

she wanted
our love life
to be
relatively simple,
except that
I was supposed to
only
be with her.

asleep on my chest,
she never dreamed
anything
beautiful.

awake,
I would play
old cure songs
in my head.

during the days
I would buy
new shoes
without her permission.

I would run.

I would eat bad
hot dogs.

she doesn't know
what it means
to say,
"so just
kiss me."

second thoughts in columbus, ohio

how far is toledo
from here?

place where I was born,
I am
fond of the fact
that at least
I was conceived
in new york.

I live in brooklyn now.

trying to put together
a healthy
body of writing
that I can be proud of.

trying to act in films.

some girls
want to spend six hours
a day
with me,
when I can only afford two.

it's hard
being me.

I can't get married
now.

cautious

I don't call
mayanna,
because
I am only
physically
attracted
to her.

I'm afraid
that
she'd try
and talk
to me
when
you know
what I
really
want.

the dark bells

are probably
what
my gothic sister
hears
calling her
in the middle
of the night.

I'm sure they're
telling her
some really
crazy shit like,

"buy custom made fangs."

she's 17,
so I don't mind.

but I've seen
the twentysomething
unhealthy fat girls
with slow minds
and
I get worried.

but I have faith in
my sister.

this is just a phase (repeat 3 times).

the inertia of a lonely heart

there is no force
acting
against loneliness
or hearts.

at least,
not in the realm of
physics.

fortunately
physics does not
include love.

but chemistry does.

are you getting
my funny metaphors
now?

then decipher
bichromium fluoride,
dickface.

that wasn't a nice word
to write,
but I'm alone
in the world
and can take
certain liberties.

collect beads of night

this is probably
some other thing
that has
to do with
gothic america
that I don't
know about.

I'd better call my
little sister
in long island
about this.

she's probably
an expert
on the subject.

communion

I was 14,
may-lee was 12,
and melody
was 9.

my mother decided
that it was time
for the three of us
to really start
becoming catholic.

this would lead me
to kissing edie
at the confirmation retreat.

later that year,
may-lee would
kill herself.

that made my father
turn catholic.

actually,
I don't know
what made my dad
decide to become
catholic.

maybe it was my mom again.

because may-lee
never killed herself.

love poem

I want
you
now.

do not think
about this.

we are in love.

if we die
tonight,
we
might as well
be having
the greatest sex
of our lives.

with each other,
of course.

father of a deaf girl

I guess that would be
jessica harden's dad
from my old
junior high school days.

I never saw the guy,
but I'm sure she told
him the same thing
when he stared
at her
perfect breasts.

I'm deaf,
not blind.

dionne & I

I do not
call her psychic line.

I feel that
she was unsuccessful
in convincing me
during her
commercial.

maybe if she sang
or something
I'd be
persuaded to
call.

I'm not that busy
in life.

1B

I hear apartment 1B
has sexy college girls
living in it.

I often walk by
thinking
about what's
behind that front door.

I keep thinking about
introduction scenarios.

I keep thinking about
possible four ways.

I keep thinking about
noises.

but here I am,
in the early afternoon,
two floors up,
not moving
a single muscle
in
their direction.

the slow migration of glaciers

you are big
and cold
and all you do
is sit
in the dark,
waiting
to destroy things.

I don't think
that's a healthy
way
for a fat girl
to live.

bitterness suits no one.

tai pei

being famous
isn't important.

unless it somehow
gets you
in contact
with your
true love.

why hasn't jewel
called me?

tai pei 2

I was never meant for anyone
in my eyes.

all of my relationships
seemed like
perfect compromises.

I don't mind
having to
still keep looking
for fire.

most men die
unhappy.

most women, too.

tai pei 3

in the mall
I saw
the most beautiful girl
walking
hand in hand
with her
little brother.

too young for me,
I wondered
who she talked to
on the phone
at night.

I wondered if she
was
one of those
smart kids
who takes
geometry
in the eighth grade.

long legs.

I walked into
barnes & noble
cursing
my age.

in the south of england somewhere

I imagine
my friend saul
becoming
more
famous.

everyone considers him
(insert 'magical' like adjectives here),
even me.

from thousands of miles away,
thank you
saul.

who knows
how fucked up
I would be
if I hadn't
met you.

1966

ten years before
I was born
and five
before
my parents even
set foot in america.

in the humid phillippines,
coconuts,
cock fights,
and
oceans

always oceans.

my most beautiful mother
learning about love
from my crazy dad.

now they're both crazy
and living in
long island.

I would've loved
to see them dancing, dancing
with
no kids
waiting for them
at home.

a couple sitting on a bench

I am not the man
sitting on the bench

and I wonder
what such a beautiful
woman
is doing
with the man
who is sitting on the bench.

I am angry over nothing.

thank you, dad.

envy

in the shower
I see that
all the other swimmers
have a couple of inches
on me.

I am the greatest writer of all time!

pretty

doesn't mean shit.

give me heart
and
laughter
all night long.

I lie sometimes.

those certain girls

I am always fascinated by those
girls,
the certain ones,
you know what I mean.

the ones who walk through life
never knowing
that the only reason they get
a damn thing
is because they're beautiful.

those girls-
they depress me.

men take advantage of them.

sausages

jeremy used to go to parties
with a 3 pound pepperidge farms
and hit
'bamas on the head.

as we approach the millennium
I eagerly await
the return
of those days.

though I am 8

my cousin wants me
to play with him
outside in the bronx.

my shins are shot
from breakdancing,

my lower back
was always weak,

my lungs are
having a hard time.

he keeps running
and running.

michael,
never grow up.

dylan

I caused his heart to break
the summer
we were 17.

his girlfriend cheated on him
with me
and
then broke up with him
because of it.

he cried for a long time
at my house.

to this day,
it's possible
that he still
doesn't know.

I'm sorry.

vincent said

that saul was great
in the movie *slam*.

saul said
he would go see
buffalo 66.

vincent laughed,
looked at
the model
in the third row
of the press conference
and invited

me and saul
to a party.

we didn't go.

vincent will never know
what we did that night.

like he cares about our friendship.

camouflage

I tape
branches and leaves
to my body
and hide
behind the bushes
used as landscaping
outside of
public pools.

waiting quietly for
the perfect moment
to drop a
baby ruth
into the water.

sara said

that there was
an 'h'
at the end of her name.

I figured
that this was
some kind of
sign
that we were
starting on
the wrong foot.

we ended up becoming
great high school friends,
though.

when was the last time
I spoke to her?

three years ago?

marc tells me she's got a baby
and isn't married.

I'm not seeing anyone
and am living with
three guys.

things change.
(this is not the end
of the poem)

sara was one of the many
oklahoma girls
that never fell in love with me,
but always loved me.

I miss these girls for some reason.

I feel like
writing long letters.

parking lot

at the state swim meet
we snuck out
and tipi'd
the rival high school's
bus.

being freshmen,
it was the great thrill
of the season.

that night
I came in my hand
for about the 100th time.

the next morning
I didn't swim so well.

damn these hands.

coffee shop

I used to hang out
at medina's
on wednesdays
in oklahoma.

last on the
open mic,
wild-eyed and skinny
(oh, to be skinny!)
I learned
about limits.

always trying to
pick up girls.

all girls at arms length.

love poetry
is in no equations
for
getting laid.

look at me now.

I say to you idols

I am not
going to
be fond
of writing
that I
am not
fond of.

steady yourself

if you do not prepare
for the kick,

you will not be able
to hit your target
with the gun.

guns have kick.

at target ranges
I learned how to hit
a human head
from 100 yd.

I swear to you,
they were not
my guns
I was using,

but what can you learn
at a gun range?

what can you gain
by being out there,
earplugged
and goggled,
firing at paper?

there is a poem
for everything.

this is not a statement
on society.

awaken, love

we enjoy these coke slurpies
in virginia,
killing time
before *the truman show.*

last night
in bed,
we came together
again.

that's a very hard thing
to do,
but we seem to be
very good at it.

you're good at
all of the things
I want
someone to be good at.

except for
buying sneakers.

that's why
we're madly
in love
with each other.

that's why
I kiss you
on the subway
in new york.

that's why
we don't
tell our parents
about
each other.

we are pure.

gather yourself

up from
your first failure.

now
is the time
to succeed.

you

are not my first love.

you do not
remind me
of my mother.

you leak
that which
makes other
people
soft.

in the fall
you look like
someone
about to burst
into flame.

I type poems
for you
that no one else
will ever see.

you sing to me
in italian.

we drink margaritas
when we get silly.

sometimes
we have
unprotected sex
and
it's ok.

bleary eyed

wipe the boogers
from your eyes
and put
your contacts
back in.

now look at me
and tell me
what
we're going to do
with our lives.

today is the last day
of
the chuck close exhibit
and tomorrow
is the full moon.

you're the girl
I would've given
my 8 by 10
elementary school photo
to.

you love my new shoes.

I'm going to
make you
come
so hard
tonight.

I miss your touch

playing water polo,
I was the defender.

how many kicked thighs
or clawed ribs
did we experience?

we went to
junior nationals
together.

do you remember
ft. lauderdale?

teaching me
how to
fake a foul.

teaching me
how to
steal.

those days
are behind us.

night falls

on my shoulders
and weighs me down.

I will
great writing
out of my fingertips.

but the moon
brings women
to my door
and forces
idiocy out of me.

wild nights
of fun,

that is what I call it.

to be
in the arms
of someone
with
no responsible
thought
in your mind
whatsoever.

eat cheesecake.

we have been called

chinese
when our backs
are turned,
sister.

guess what?

we are chinese.

in new york,
that's a bonus
for women
and gay men.

I'm straight.

underage

she didn't know
how I could
break her heart
after we had fallen
so hard
for each other.

just because she was 15,
didn't make me
more mature.

I left her for a fling with a manhattan
model,
underweight from cocaine
and not eating.

that's how stupid
naïve
oklahoma boys can be
upon first arriving
in new york.

grimshaw

sounds a lot like
grimlock,
      the dinobot.

I used to call her grimlock
when I was really drunk.

grimshaw
is her last name.

she is my daddy's
little secret.

born of adultery.

I used to fuck her
on visits
to vermont (her home).

just because
a poem
is a big lie
doesn't mean
that it doesn't
mean anything.

a slow disease

giving up on your dreams,
but not committing
suicide.

all the words

are locked in a secret vault
that only special midgets
appointed by god
can access.

they are the little friends
that writers keep
in their homes
for the express purpose
of lending them words
to write great things with.

they are paid handsomely.

some midgets
even have their own
horses.

miniature ones, of course.

you are not

as bitter
as I once
thought you
to be.

I guess you just have
a real big chip
on your shoulder.

if you would just
let go
every
once in awhile,
I bet you would
feel
a lot better.

come on,
kristyn.

at 19, you shouldn't
have to even think
bed time.

the strip 1

she wanted
to show me
the dance she does
at sassy merlot's.

we had had
bad sex
six times already.

I was 19,
it was summer,
and it seemed cool
to be lying down
while
an older woman
stripped
in front of you.

later, we had bad sex
again.

in the bathtub
I learned
that sex
isn't good
unless it is.

the strip 2

I thought
that after being
on the boardwalk,
holding hands,
she would
take me home
and teach me
about how
a woman
can love a man.

she didn't know
a damn thing
and the
music she played
while
we were
doing it
sucked.

shush

do not say
another horny word
or
I'm going
to come.

I'm serious.

that's not funny.
no

don't
touch
my balls,
either.

I am not from here

earthlings,
I have traveled 2 gillion lit yerons
to see your planet.

I would like
to try one of your milkshakes.

and also,
I would like
a cheeseburger.

infatuation

I don't know
if it was because
her name
was genevieve,
but
I really
was into
this girl.

I forget how old she must be
now,
but she was
two years
older than me
when I met her.

tan and skinny
and perky
in the tit area,
baby boy dakota
always at home-

I adored her.

she laughed at my jokes
and danced with me
at the club in oklahoma.

we were rave kids.

that was a long time
ago.

the fall

she was not
lying to me
when she said
that we
do not belong
to each other.

so why was I
hurt

when I woke up
only to find
that she was not
next to me,
but was upstairs,
naked and drunk
in bed with chad?

I will never
let a girl
take me
to stay
at a friend's house
when I know
that he
wants to
fuck her.

ouch.

long has a cloak

that he wears
to the black horde meetings.

as minister of propaganda
he decides
what mischievious
things
the black horde
will be doing
on any given night.

the cloak holds evil spirits
of those who
killed virgins

and long
has a really
scary
voice.

mercy

now that you have me
handcuffed
to the bed,

I hope that you're
kind enough
not to
shit on me
or
take a big dildo
and fuck me
with it.

many people died
during
the bataan death march.

compass

alawrence
used it
to get around
during the
beginning
of the movie.

later, as he became one
with all of the tribes of
arabia,
there was no
need for it.

I thought I'd tell you
what the movie
was about
so that
you wouldn't have to spend
four hours watching it.

though it is
the most
beautiful thing.

freedom

I can write
whatever I want.

even if it is
an exercise,
like this book.

plus,
I have
nothing
to prove.

road spent

trekking cross country
to my uncle's
in the bronx
with my best friend
marc
was a great trip.

coming back
I realized
that we could
never
live together.

I will not be able
to get those days back,
so I'm glad
they were spent
so well.

one day,
I won't be able
to sit on a stoop
and go unnoticed
as people walk by.

I'm glad I have spent
my days so well.

christmas in hawaii

we were about to do it
when we realized
that we didn't have
any condoms.

we went down on each other
instead.

chinese like me,
there was something
potent about it
just because of that.

afterwards she talked
about her parents in hawaii.

they owned a jewelry store.

she had a beautiful back
and graduated college
the same year
I did.

spoiled

when
rachel neglected to
tickle my anus
during intercourse,
I was so shocked
that I used it
as just cause to
break up.

later in life
I learned not to
be so critical
of women
who are not of
new york, la,

        or spain.

red light district, amsterdam

there seems to be
a lot of cool things
going on
somewhere else
in the world.

I bet some prostitute
in amsterdam
wishes
that she had
my life.

I often wished
that I could live
other people's lives.

what is today?
who
am I?

writing all of these poems
at once
is making me
crazy.

lovers for lilly

after lydia
and marc broke up
she started
having sex
with a bunch
of guys.

marc began working
on a novel.

this summer she's
in san francisco,
probably
learning more
about love.

she promised to sleep with me
if I visited her.

oh, the pressure.

I just want to
remember her
as my best friend's
beautiful girlfriend
and
stay home.

lemonade

in our back yard
in brooklyn
we
talk about
summer girlfriends.

by july
we will all be
crazy.

june are the days
we drink
pink lemonade
and watch
the sun set.

we talk

sometimes.

mostly
I think
that we
do best
in bed.

you are a socialist
and I
am a capitalist
and it's very
hard for us
to say
anything
to each other
without

throwing things.

actually, upon further examination
I don't think
that I am a capitalist,

but I am certainly not
a
communist or a socialist.

that's you.

we should just
have sex.

spivey leaks

from his pores
like a
creature
in a bad
horror movie.

he wonders
why
he doesn't
get laid.

I'm afraid to tell him
that it's
because
he has
a low IQ.

forgetful

was I
in love with you?

you count the number
of receipts
you have
each month,
then put each month's receipts
in an envelope
and label them.

when you get your period
you say things
about your past.

I have always let
my mother
cut my hair.

lost

all of the dark children
of the night

can basically be thrust
into this category
if I so desire,

because I am
the author

and kids don't like
to read
or write
nowadays,

so who's gonna
argue with me?

my little sister?

she's reading *tales of
vampire erotica.*

I doubt we'll ever have
a social issue debate.

still life

two breasts

asleep on my bed.

b cups that are tan
and perfect.

I kiss the left nipple
which hardens
shortly after.

I whisper,
"dear god,"

while anna
dreams
about a viking ship
and red-haired men
burning
mountain villages.

I don't suppose raindrops

only one girl I kissed
did not love the rain.

they were all still crazy,
though.

that's why
poems about the rain
work so well
on a woman's thighs.

we all aspire to learn
more
about clouds.

sometimes

I get hard
thinking about
a woman's
perfect ass.

sometimes
I write
things
and weeks later,
can't remember
if I
wrote it.

sometimes
I go out to eat
with my sister.

sometimes
I take my centrum.

sometimes
I get depressed.

terribly, terribly
depressed.

blanketed by a citrus smile

eating oranges
during half time
of a second grade
soccer game
and lauren
offers me the last slice,
while

eating one.

I take it and smile.
she smiles back,
swallows,
and tells me
that I am a good
defender.

the road

is a place
where I get to think
more noble things
than usual.

I listen to really great music,
driving the speed limit,
passing through
towns I am familiar with.

I think better
driving through
towns
I'm familiar with.

the road is a bucket.

explain that.

I guess what I wanted was

true love,
but really drunk
and alone
at three
in the morning
I fucked you
anyway.

when we woke up
I could not deny
that you were
beautiful.

I do not want to say
bad things
about you
in my poetry.

insecurity

when a 25 year old
goes out
with a 15 year old
and knows
exactly why.

I am patient

I will be here
until you
understand me.

then I will leave.

the things you fear

pregnancy, subversive literature,
nike,
death, cancer, AIDS, crabs,
your mother,
riding lawn mowers.

the chase

I used peripheral vision
to look at her
for seventeen minutes
in
barnes & noble.

she moved closer
by picking up magazines
on the way
to me.

I smiled in a different
direction
when she glanced over.

she caught me
looking at her,
then kept looking.

I walked by and smiled.

she followed.

I walked out the door
and
never
saw her
again.

fragile

when someone doesn't know
why the hell
they're
losing
their virginity.

I'm writing to tell you

that I want
the 300 dollars
that you owe me,
or I'm sicking
my lawyer
on your sorry
asses.

you think it's funny
that you can blow off
a little guy like me.

well I'm not the
coke head bimbo
you fuck at night.

I'm beau sia.

watch out.

and so to receive you

I take a shower
and masturbate.

put on my issey miyake
and easy-
to-get-out-of
clothes.

I clean my room
and make sure
the bed
doesn't have
anything
incriminating
on it.

I select music.

I make sure
you walk in
seeing things
that show
I'm worth it.

I prepare jokes
in my head.

I drink some
iced tea
before
brushing my teeth.

fat

that's what you are,
so
kill yourself.

junky

that's what she
used to be
until
she had a baby.

now she's a
better writer
than me.

austin, tx, sheraton hotel, 2 a.m.

did I stay the night here
once
during a
water polo
meet,

or did we drive home
the same day?

my memories move
even when
they don't.

I keep expecting you to

run into my bedroom naked
and tell me
to take you.

I feel like we're on the verge
of doing crazy
wonderful things together.

carriage rides through central park

swimming in the ocean
on cold days

sex sex and more sex in more sex sex ways!

I keep thinking that
you will be here
on my birthday
and give me
a present no one's
given me
before.

take my picture.

this is what we look like
wild.

p.s.

I really
don't like
jack kerouac
or
the way
you give
blowjobs.

gold fish

one of the many pets
that I
never had.

new moon

is when gothic girls
like my sister melody

go outside
and sacrifice stupid things
like dolls
to gods
they've named themselves,

hoping to somehow
get something
like
vampire powers or something.

I wish *the crow*
was never made.

someone to know me

I just want to spend time
with you
and hopefully
we will
really get
to know
each other.

buy my CD.

traffic

you are the girl
I was talking about
in the poem 'fat.'

please jump into traffic
and kill yourself.

now.

home

you want me
to be
the first.

I don't think
that I can
deal
with that kind of
responsibility.

this is why
I am taking
you home
now.

after the divorce

you said
that we were
going to move
to england.

you said
that I would get to
go to a school
where
all I would learn
was painting.

wait a minute.

you and dad
never got divorced.

everyone
does not live
the same life.

isn't that great?

may brought longer days

are you going
to ever sing to me
again?

we have been sorry
for over a year now
and
keep punching
each other
through the bad letters
that we write.

if I ever write more than
a page to you
I know this dumb love
will be resolved
and you will
move here
to live with me.

we just need to pick
a song to call
our song.

and we need to
sleep together
without
thinking of
other people.

get john camey
out of your mind.

in exchange,
you can take off
my ex-girlfriend mask.

crazy cow

I would call you this,
except I would
replace 'crazy'
with 'fat.'

you're the girl from
'fat'
and 'traffic.'

if you're not dead
yet,
then I have failed.

sauna

morgan and I hopped
into his apartment complex
sauna
during spring break.

when we hopped out
two girls
were looking at us
very naughtily.

morgan has always been
very charming
and that night
we ate
and slept with them.

my girl's name
was yvette.

this is all
a silly lie.

the tangled roots of willows

is a subject
I'm not too
familiar with.

what I am familiar with
is when
I wake up
and have
an erection.

goodness
(a poem for shane)

you and andy hicks
never liked me
that much.

you were the good 'ol boys
of our high school.

may you always
remain oblivious.

wolves in the canyon

I could never write a poem
about wolves in the canyon,
so don't
expect me to.

god exists quietly

inside my underwear.

why don't you come over
and say hello?

miracle

all pussies
in the universe
suddenly
only
fit me.

beau's short version life

originally from Central Outworld Ott Six Ott, beau has managed to infiltrate New U.S.A East through subverting many genetic things. since moving to our airy fortress above the Outworld scum which infect our pure society, beau has managed to publish several things, including *this is the pussy light* and *revolution is in my hands now... and right now my hands are busy jacking off.* winner of the 1998 southern california greatest writer of all time poetry prize, beau is also the recipient of many non-governmental grants including the rich-old-women-that-he-fucks-for-money grant and the-rich-old-gay-white-men-that-he-cleans-their-houses-naked-for-money grant. not to be outdone by charles bukowsky, mr. sia constantly boasts about the number of boils he has to have drained daily. finally, beau has a very rare form of a terminal disease that can only be cured by the adult way of loving from sexy women who have high media exposure. blue is his favorite color.

Enjoy Beau's book? Don't miss his debut CD...

ATTACK!
ATTACK!
GO!

"A bug out!" – *Spin*

"Hilarious!" – *New York Times*

At finer record and book stores everywhere
or phone 1-800-992-6731

Produced by Sam Sever and Jonathan Hoffman
for Fuzzy Logic Productions

**mouth
almighty
records**